Getting started in the puzzling world
of cryptocurrency

MICHAEL LEWIS, MD

Copyright © 2018 by Willow Bay Press
All rights reserved. This book or any portion thereof
may not be reproduced or used in any manner whatsoever
without the express written permission of the publisher
except for the use of brief quotations in a book review.

Printed in the United States of America

First Printing, 2018

ISBN-13: 978-0692196137 (Willow Bay Press)
ISBN-10: 0692196137

Willow Bay Press
7842 Valley Flores Dr.
West Hills, CA
91304

www.WillowBayPress.com

To my beautiful wife and partner, Jenn:
Thank you for putting up with yet another project

part 1
in the beginning

What Is Cryptocurrency?
Cryptography

CRYPTOGRAPHY IS THE ABILITY TO KEEP THINGS SECRET or safe by using encryption so that falsification and theft are almost impossible. Then by definition, cryptocurrency is a digital asset that is encrypted to generate units of currency and be transferred independently of a regulated system such as banks, thus giving cryptocurrency its claim to fame as a "decentralized" coin. But what about the crypto- part of the currency? All currencies, wallets, exchanges (all to be discussed later) are protected by two keys: a private key and a public key. These keys are made up of a series of numbers and letters which are specific to the individual owner and cannot be hacked, for example:

0x6d8ad04a86d9cc1cae3281234xxowpm56789101827663b5e1a33220498f2f81ced9e3d8

The private key is a unique key that *only you* should have, while the public key, though unique as well, is shared in every transaction. The very presence of one key validates the existence of the other, yet one is secure while the other is not.

Think of it like this. Imagine a locked cage (wallet), containing an imaginary homing pigeon, which delivers messages where you tell it to go. This imaginary pigeon also has an imaginary marker around its neck with a small engraving which reads, "Billy Smith's key" – this is your public key. For the homing pigeon to deliver the message, the cage must be unlocked by the only key in existence, the private key. Once opened (transaction requested), the pigeon can deliver the message to the receiver (an exchange or wallet). The receiver knows the message is from Billy Smith because it is verified by the public key that is around the pigeon's neck, therefore can be validated and accepted.

If you want to make a transaction and send Bitcoin (a cryptocurrency) to an exchange to purchase other cryptocurrencies (to be discussed later), you must tell the entity that is housing your money how much you want to send and where it will be delivered (the pigeon's message). Once you click *send* (validating the private key), you essentially open the cage and release the pigeon. Obviously, it's a bit more complex than that because there has to be something keeping track of all these pigeons or it would be chaos. This is where the ledger comes in, a.k.a., the blockchain.

The Blockchain

THE BLOCKCHAIN IS A DIGITAL LEDGER that accounts for the time, the amount, the deposit address and the public key of each transaction that has *ever been made*. So just how big is it? As of the date of writing this book, the blockchain is 154 Gigabytes (GB). To put that into perspective, our DNA contains 100 times less information (in Gigabytes) than the data encrypted on the blockchain. What's more, the blockchain contains 100 times more data in transactions than data present in the entire Encyclopedia Britannica and produces over 200,000 transactions daily. Other blockchains, such as Etherium, are growing similarly.

TO FIRST UNDERSTAND THIS CURRENCY, one must first define what *currency* is. Currency is an agreement between people that a specific unit has a particular value. Think of it like this: When you were a child you probably owned trading cards. In my case, it was Garbage Pail Kids. Most would agree that card 8a of the first series was the most sought-after card as long as it was in mint condition (this card was "Adam Bomb" for those who care or want to remember). Well, let's say that Billy, your neighbor, really wanted that card and was willing to trade his 1986 Diamond-Back bicycle with front-frame pegs for your mint condition, 8a Adam Bomb card. Because Billy sees this card as tradeable, and has an agreed upon value (1 Bike equals one GPK 8a Card) it is now considered a currency. If you think this sounds like a trade, then you would be correct because a trade is nothing more than swapping one thing for another of a perceived equivalent value, such as $1.99 for a 20oz Cola Bottle, or $11,000 for 1 Bitcoin.

The security system built into the blockchain is tight! It is much more secure than any Fiat (paper money) bank or credit card institution. People steal credit cards and cheat banks all the time, so what's to stop people from theft on the blockchain? First, because the bank is a centralized entity, all the information is stored in one place making theft much simpler. The ledger or Blockchain is made up of people all over the world maintaining the ledger with their personal computers or networks. These people are referred to as "miners" because for every transaction that is validated, Bitcoins are released into the network, similar to how mining gold works, only digitally (more on this shortly). To be a miner, you have to have a robust (expensive) computer with high-end video cards and significant cooling, which then, of course, drives your electricity costs way up. So, why would people do this? Well, this is the genius behind it— The owner of the node (or specific part of the ledger) receives Bitcoin fractions for each transaction that s/he validates. Therefore, the more you mine, the more Bitcoin you make.

Don't be fooled because if you think that you can mine bitcoin, make a stack of money and retire from your nine-to-five, think again because you need many computers and lots of money just to make small returns. I should also mention that people don't have to own entire Bitcoins because the currency was designed so that people can hold small fractions of it (Some out to the 8th decimal place!). For example:

$$100 \text{ USD} = 0.0145521556 \text{ BTC}$$
(at exchange current rate)

Once a transaction becomes a part of the ledger, the node computer has to perform a sequence of math problems for the transaction to become valid. These are called Hash functions. Once these complex math problems are solved, the transaction is now considered a block on the ledger. When a series of Hash functions have been solved we get chains of blocks, hence the "Block-chain." Most transactions require 2 to 6 Hash functions to be solved for a currency to be delivered to the wallet or exchanges and be validated. It's a necessary check and balance system and can take minutes to hours for the transaction to be validated.

No Chip Poker

Let's say you are at a poker game and someone forgot to bring the poker chips. So, each person pulls out a pen and a piece of paper to keep track of the money won and lost for each hand. At the end of each hand, everyone cross-references each other's papers (the ledger) and compares the outcomes. Due to the individual oversight, the players can catch inaccuracies (perform basic hash functions) before it becomes part of the *final* ledger. Once everyone agrees on the results of each hand, the transaction is validated. Only then can the player receive their winnings. The paper is set aside, and this hand is considered closed (a block on the ledger)! At the end of the game, the pile of closed hands is now considered *a chain of blocks*–a listing of all transactions that took place during the poker game. Yes, a blockchain

So why have a decentralized currency?

IN A CENTRALIZED SYSTEM, FIAT CURRENCY is highly regulated yet can be easily manipulated by the Government. Maybe you are thinking that the government prevents this kind of manipulation and volatility. For the most part that is true. But in 2008 when the USA housing market came crashing down, many in the government, despite obvious foresight, shamefully did nothing, thus ruining the financial lives of many. This topic is complex and no one entity is fully to blame, but understand that Government manipulation, whether direct or indirect, occurs more often than we see.

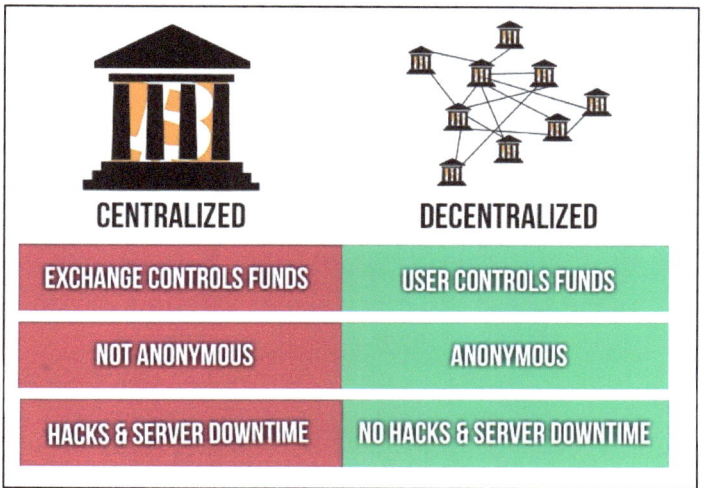

Who's Backing the Bills!

The United States Mint, with permission from the Congress, prints and backs each dollar that they produce. Essentially, this means that the Government is guaranteeing the $20 that you have in your wallet. Since there is Government backing the currency, it's worth is widely understood and therefore now acceptable for trade, such as a gallon of milk at your local grocery store for a fraction of that $20. If the Government disappeared tomorrow the dollar would plummet because no single entity is there to vouch for its worth. At the same time, the US Government can print more money on demand worsening our total debt and devaluing our dollar, just like what happened in 2009 in Zimbabwe.

The 100 Trillion Dollar Note

IN THE MID-1990s REGULATIONS IN ZIMBABWE were causing significant land reforms for farmers. The Government was taking away land from white farmers and redistributing it to black farmers who had little to no experience in farming. Due to this governmental decision, farms failed, crops died, and food production fell over 45%. Both agricultural and manufacturing declined leading to a significant collapse in bank lending. To make up for this, the government, using their own money-making-copy-machine, began printing money. At the same time, soldiers were demanding more pay, while they faced a current war in the Congo. This was the beginning of the demise. As debt increased, the Government printed more money, causing more inflation, which caused business owners to raise prices on goods and services anticipating a windfall of money, since more money was expected to pour into their economy. However, with more printing and a shortage of goods, prices rose dramatically. Their currency became so weak that they printed a $100 Trillion note:

People became "poverty billionaires," which wasn't a good thing especially if you made 1 billion dollars per week and a can of soup cost 1/2 billion. Next, I will illustrate just how badly the Zimbabwean Government and dollar failed.

The "Shitty" Math:

IN THE USA, A ROLL OF TOILET PAPER COSTS about $0.86, where each roll has an average of 154 sheets (double ply). Therefore, each square of paper is $0.005 (1/2 cent-per-square)

1 Zimbabwe Dollar (ZWD) is worth $.0027 USD or about 1/4 cent-per-square.

This means it cheaper to wipe your ass with a Zimbabwe Dollar than it would be to use toilet paper. Or, 1 square of toilet paper is worth twice as much as 1 ZWD!

So, Why Won't We Use Our Cryptocurrency To Wipe Our Butts?

In cryptocurrency world, the currency is decentralized. Therefore, there isn't a single entity to print money on demand to make up for losses and devalue the currency. Bitcoin, for example, has a total MAXIMUM supply of 21,000,000 coins, with a current circulating supply of 16,841,525. There will never be anymore Bitcoin than 21,000,000. This condition will help drive the demand upwards. Experts say the last Bitcoin will be mined in 2140, interestingly which is *about the same rate that gold is mined and made available to the public.*

The $100 Million Pizzas

BITCOIN WAS THE FIRST MAJOR CRYPTOCURRENCY adopted, though it wasn't the first. There were a few before its arrival in 2009 that never were implemented or took off: B-Money and Bit-Gold. In 2008, the enigmatic Satoshi Nakamoto (a pseudonym) wrote a paper called *Bitcoin – A Peer to Peer Electronic Cash System.* It was posted to a mailing list discussion group. His true identity is still a mystery. In 2009 Bitcoin was made available to the public. At this point, mining began and transactions were being verified on the blockchain. Its initial value hadn't been determined until 2010 when the first Bitcoin was traded—*10,000 Bitcoin for two pizzas*. Seriously! At today's prices that would be worth over $100 million!

Currently, Bitcoin dominates the crypto market with a market share of 34% (of total market capitalization, to be discussed later). Bitcoin is the primary currency when purchasing alt-coins via trading pairs. Alt-coins or alternative coins, to be discussed later, are all coins which aren't Bitcoin. There are thousands of coins, many with different uses within their niche trying to solve a unique problem. Like Bitcoin (or anything else), the first to market is usually the king (or Queen)!

Satoshi Nakamoto's Abstract from his initial paper

Abstract. A purely peer-to-peer version of electronic cash would allow online payments to be sent directly from one party to another without going through a financial institution. Digital signatures provide part of the solution, but the main benefits are lost if a trusted third party is still required to prevent double-spending. We propose a solution to the double-spending problem using a peer-to-peer network. The network timestamps transactions by hashing them into an ongoing chain of hash-based proof-of-work, forming a record that cannot be changed without redoing the proof-of-work. The longest chain not only serves as proof of the sequence of events witnessed but proof that it came from the largest pool of CPU power. As long as a majority of CPU power is controlled by nodes that are not cooperating to attack the network, they'll generate the longest chain and outpace attackers. The network itself requires minimal structure. Messages are broadcast on a best effort basis, and nodes can leave and rejoin the network at will, accepting the longest proof-of-work chain as proof of what happened while they were gone.

~

Beyond Bitcoin – Alt-coins/Alt-rock

BEAR WITH ME. IN THE LATE 90s, NIRVANA, Stone Temple Pilots, and Alice in Chains inserted themselves into the music scene and created chaos amongst their rival hair bands while putting Seattle on the musical map. They created a rift in the music scene and became the wave of the future over the next ten years. These Alt-rockers changed the entire construct of music and truly and literally were "alternative." Their alternative title was more than just their music or peculiar vocal style (yarl), but in their rebellious lifestyle, clothes and simplicity of musicianship. Before we knew it, alternative rock bands seeded the scene and grew prolifically until hair metal was eventually phased out. It wasn't until a decade later when hair metal bands gave themselves a haircut and made a re-emergence doing nostalgic tours leading to further album sales. See Bon Jovi.

Shit-Coins?

MANY NEWER ALT-COINS ARE PARASITICALLY planting themselves in today's crypto plots. There are currently over 1,500 alt-coins, yet only 1 Bitcoin. Caveat Emptor because like most copy-cats, many alt-coins are not necessarily legit, or even good for that matter—similar to some 90's alt-bands. You remember the Spin-Doctors don't you?

Most believe that if one wants to make money quickly, the focus of your crypto portfolio should be alt-coins. To make money in crypto, many pay attention to the multipliers. For example, Ripple (XRP), the fastest growing cryptocurrency alt-coin in 2017 was worth $.005 (1/2 cent) per coin in February 2017 and "moon'd" to $3.69 in January 2018. That's a 738x multiplier! In other words, a $1,000 investment would've been worth $738,000 in 11 months! Bitcoin doesn't have the multipliers that the newer alt-coins have, yet still, Bitcoin remains a solid long-term investment. As far as multipliers go, if Bitcoin is at $9,000 and rises to $20,000 like it did in December 2017 that's only a 2.2x multiplier. That's pretty good, but it sure isn't 738x!

ICOs (initial coin offerings) is where the short game is (risk too), especially when it comes to multipliers. Some coins at ICO are worth fractions of a penny and have the potential for serious gains, some over 1,000x, See Dash Coin. The exciting things about alt-coins is that many have found their unique niche, solve a real-world problem and have lots of potential for making significant changes in our world.

Some coins are being used to allow users to store their human genome safely on the blockchain for medical research or doctors, some are creating new all-in-one exchange platform wallets, while others are trying to revolutionize money transfers internationally. These Alt coins are more than just wannabe Bitcoins trying to come out from under their big brother's shadow. In fact, many are breaking the Bitcoin mold all together.

RESEARCH

Where do you find the lists of Currencies?

THERE ARE PLENTY OF ONLINE CHOICES to find a coins' information, market exchanges, and their financials. Probably the most popular one is Coin Market Cap (CMC) at www.coinmarketcap.com. Like most cap listings, coins are listed in descending order from highest market capitalizations to lowest, usually showing the top 100 first. As you can imagine, Bitcoin takes the top listing. When looking at the following pictures borrowed from the CMC, one should know and reasonably understand a few definitions (which can also be found in the glossary of terms in the back of this book):

Market Cap (MC or Market Capitalization) – this is a term which defines the coin's current worth, size, and rank. It is often confused with valuation. The MC is the product of the total circulating coins/tokens etc. and the current price per unit. Market Cap = Circulating Supply X Price

24h Volume – the amount of currency that has been traded or added to the MC in the last 24 hours.

BTC Dominance –Total MC owned by Bitcoin, as a percentage of the whole crypto market.

Circulating Supply – The best approximation of the number of coins currently being traded or in circulation at any one time.

Total Supply – Total coins in existence (minus coins that have been buried or burned)

Max Supply – The best approximation of coins that will ever exist in the life of the cryptocurrency.

Coin – a cryptocurrency that can act independently.

Token – depends on another cryptocurrency to operate

Below are some figures are taken from key parts of CMC (in February 2018).

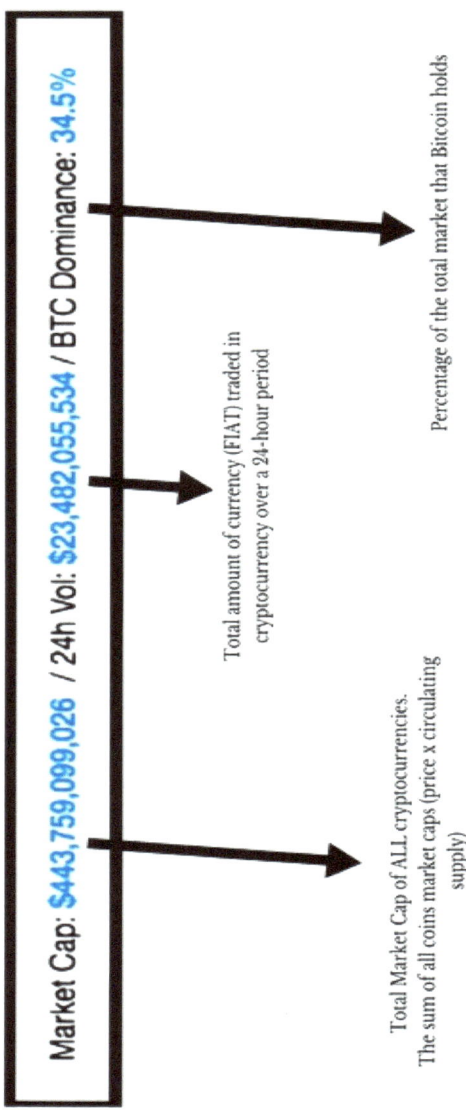

Figure 3. Basic details at the top of Coin Market Cap.

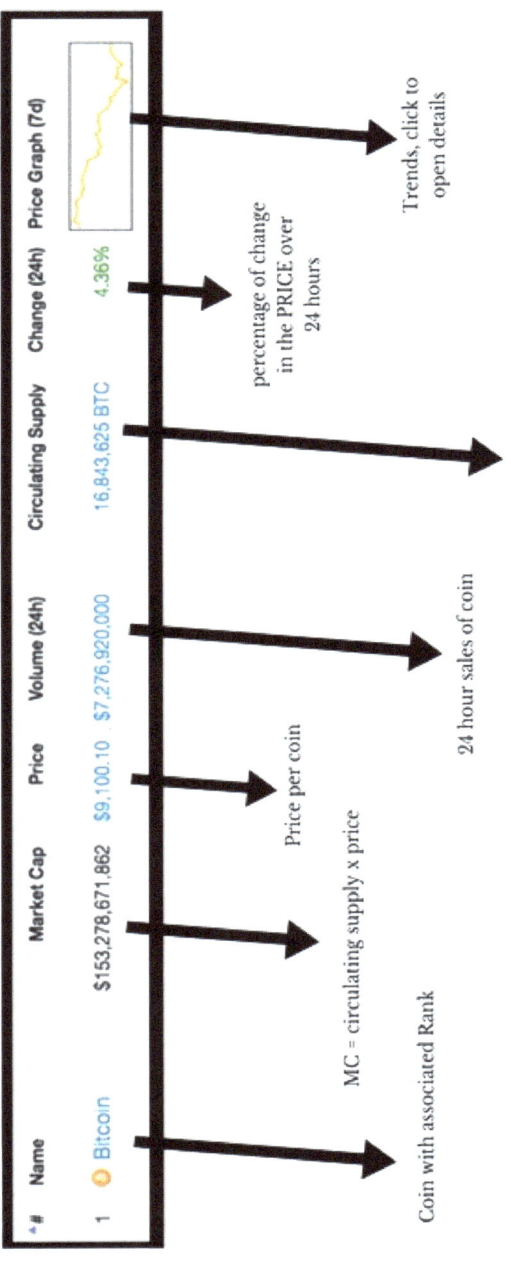

Figure 4. Listing view of details on CMC

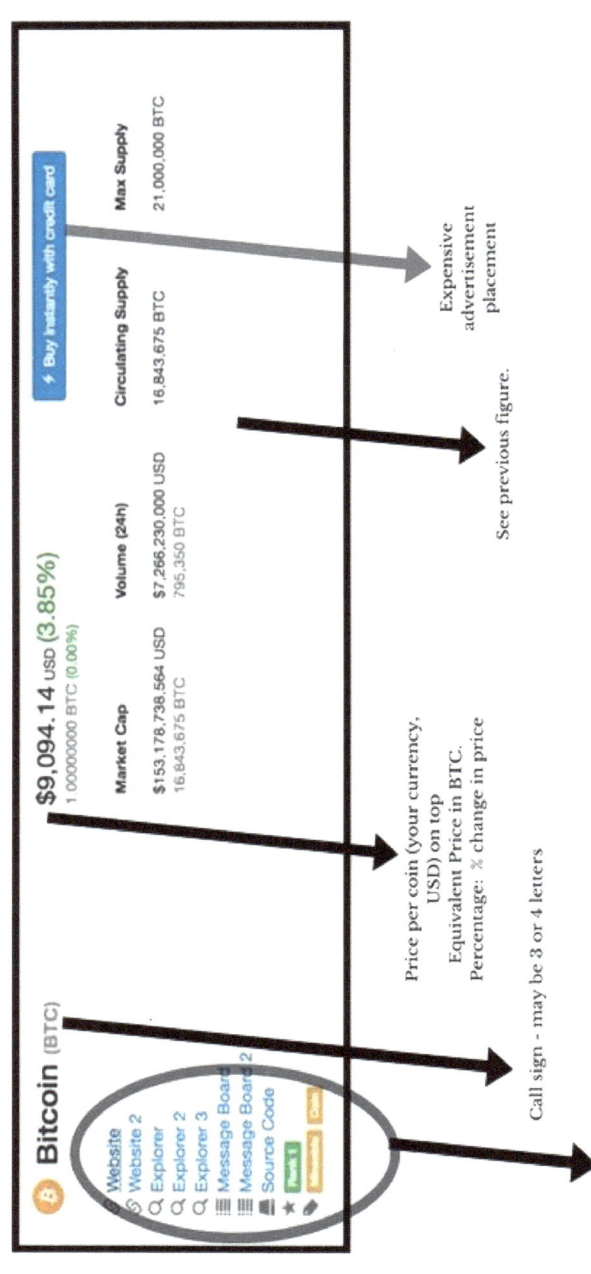

Figure 5. Higher details after clicking on coin from homepage of CMC MC

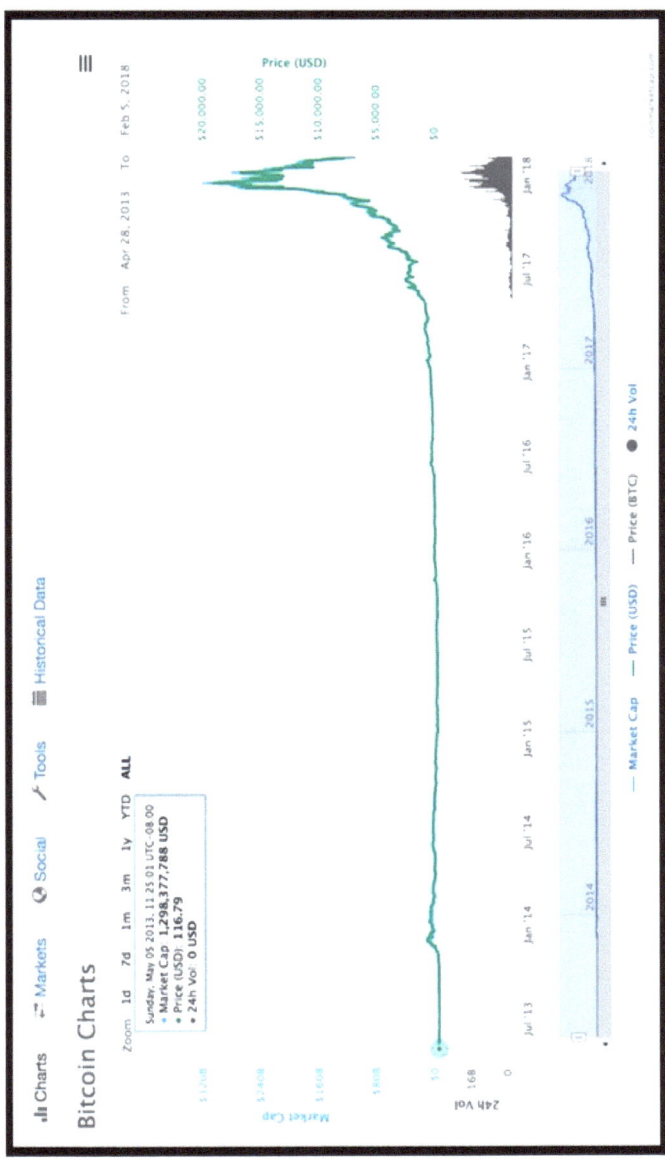

Figure 6. Just beneath the prior figure on the website, more details are found. Here is the historical chart which can be zoomed in or out based on selection or date criteria (upper right)

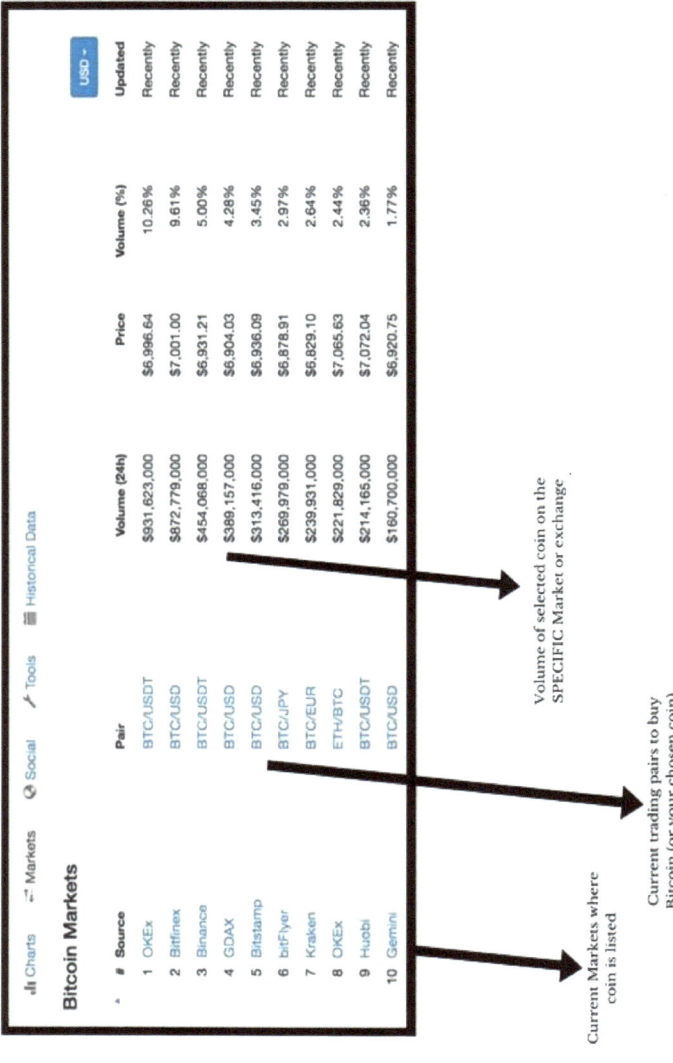

Figure 7. Same view as the prior figure but this time the MARKET tab was checked. This current view shows the top 10 markets which are trading the current chosen coin.

DEALING WITH SPECULATION AND FUD

"Buy on the rumor and sell on the news."

JUST LIKE POLITICS, "FAKE" NEWS stories are pervasive and spread FUD (Fear, Uncertainty, and Doubt) in the crypto market. However, there are reliable resources for crypto, which try to titrate out the FUD and over-speculative comments that frequently find its way into the crypto-circle.

Most of the fluctuations that take place in the market occur due to fear. Rumors generate uncertainty, which causes drops and crashes (bear markets), whereas confidence creates rises and gains (bull markets). The latest crypto crash lasting from Late January 2018 – July 2018 was thought to be initiated when the South Korean government placed a Ban on selling and trading cryptocurrency. A considerable share of cryptocurrency resides in Asian countries, and therefore the fear that the market would tank, if banned, was speculated to be imminent. This concern became a self-fulfilled prophecy and tanked the market. Interestingly, it wasn't a simply a South Korean ban that caused the crash–it was the fearful traders responding to the speculation that did. Isn't that ironic?!

There are plenty of resources to find information and news about crypto. I will list some below. Remember, the best way to filter through the vast amounts of information is to read multiple sources and make the best possible decision.

Lists of resources:

Online Objective Coin Details:

www.coinmarketcap.com

www.coincap.io (similar to CMC)

Online News Organization

Coindesk (www.coindesk.com) - a general cryptocurrency news site. The largest bitcoin news media site in the world, it is highly rated as you can get all sorts of useful information from here.

Cointelegraph (www.cointelegraph.com) - Probably the second largest news source in the bitcoin space. Mostly focused on Bitcoin and Etherium.

Social

Reddit (there are plenty of bitcoin and Alt-Coin Reddit groups.

YouTube Look for popular YouTubers and check out the number of subscribers. (Who is popping up in your search results?)

Twitter - Specific Company's Twitter feed is a big source for the latest information

Facebook – Specific Company's Facebook page may have some great information

(Twitter still likely the best option)

Discord – A peer to peer discussion group about coins – usually you can request

An invitation –this will be found on the company-specific website

Telegraph – Another peer to peer discussion app, similar to discord (somewhat).

(The company will let people know on their website if a telegraph site is available).

Exchanges / Markets:

LET'S GO SHOPPING, SHALL WE? Say you want to purchase three pairs of shoes. The first one is found at both Nordstrom's and Foot Locker. The second pair is only found at Macy's, while the third pair is only at Nordstrom. All prices are presumed to be similar:

Nordstrom's	*Macy's*	*Foot Locker*
Pair 1		*Pair 1*
	Pair 2	
Pair 3		

Based on this information, the most-efficient way to purchase ALL 3 shoes would be to buy from Nordstrom's and Macy's, correct? We can see this because both Pair 1 and 3 are at Nordstrom's and Pair 2 is only at Macy's. Let's assume that in order to purchase any pair of shoes, you need to sign-up at each store by verifying your personal and payment information in case there is a problem. So, to purchase all three pairs, you will have to open two accounts, one at Nordstrom's and the other at Macy's. This shopping analogy is similar to how crypto-markets work. There isn't one store (market or exchange) that stocks every alt-coin that you may want. If you only want to buy Bitcoin (BTC), Etherium (ETH), Litecoin (LTC) then this isn't a problem because most exchanges have these readily available to purchase when you trade your home currency in for crypto, but more on this later. However, if you are looking to buy a coin that isn't on a wallet, you will have to open an account on an exchange and send your bitcoin (in most cases) from your wallet to an exchange. Once your Bitcoin is deposited on your exchange, you now have to trade your bitcoin for the coin of your choosing—think again about the shoe analogy above.

MARKETS AND EXCHANGES:

SO, WHICH EXCHANGE SHOULD YOU CHOOSE? The answer should seemingly be, whichever exchange has your product and has the best security. If you are lucky enough to find all of your alt-coins on one exchange, that's excellent work, but now you have to worry about the safety of your hard earned money. Though fraud doesn't happen very often, you still have to be reasonably meticulous from where you purchase your currency. In 2011, MtGOX was a massive Bitcoin exchange company that was hacked and 850,000 Bitcoin were taken. Investigations are still pending. Fortunately, at least one thing came from this devastating loss: A higher priority on security and consumer awareness. This awareness has led to better and more secure, trustworthy exchanges. To determine which exchanges are most secure and reliable, we should be looking at the exchange's 24–hour trading volume. See below for trading volume as denoted by, Volume (24h) and Volume (%).

Ethos Markets

📊 Charts   ↕ Markets   🌐 Social   🔧 Tools   📅 Historical Data

USD ▾

#	Source	Pair	Volume (24h)	Price	Volume (%)	Updated
1	Binance	BQX/BTC	$4,894,820	$4.15	68.62%	Recently
2	Binance	BQX/ETH	$2,108,380	$4.17	29.56%	Recently
3	HitBTC	BQX/ETH	$48,046	$4.33	0.67%	Recently
4	CoinExchange	ETHOS/BTC	$42,806	$4.17	0.60%	Recently
5	CoinExchange	ETHOS/ETH	$17,466	$3.94	0.24%	Recently
6	Cobinhood	ETHOS/ETH	$8,371	$4.10	0.12%	Recently
7	Cobinhood	ETHOS/BTC	$4,845	$4.62	0.07%	Recently
8	EtherDelta	BQX/ETH	$4,113	$4.65	0.06%	Recently
9	Livecoin	ETHOS/BTC	$2,264	$3.85	0.03%	Recently
10	Livecoin	ETHOS/ETH	$1,063	$4.78	0.01%	Recently
11	Radar Relay	ETHOS/WETH	$610	$4.09	0.01%	Recently

Now, just because there happens to be a lower volume in some other exchanges doesn't mean that you shouldn't purchase from them, it just means the other sources are more popular - think Macy's vs small clothing outlet. Focusing on the previous figure's 24h Volume, let's assume that you did *not* have a Binance or HitBTC account, which have the highest 24h volume, but you do have a CoinExchange account. Since you may prefer to keep all of your coins in as few exchanges as possible, you may decide not to open an exchange with the higher volume just to keep things simple. Most importantly, make sure you do some research on Reddit, Google or other sources for reviews that discuss issues about legitimacy and fraud before sending your currency to an exchange. Once again, think back to the shoe analogy—you want to make your purchasing experience as efficient as possible by purchasing from a few stores as possible.

-STOP-

BEFORE MAKING ANY TRADES, You Should **DYOR** (Do Your Own Research):

Reputation – The best way to find out about an exchange is to search through reviews from individuals, Social Networks, and popular industry websites like Reddit.

Fees – Many exchanges will have withdrawal or transfer fees, so check out the FAQ section to see how much. Some fees can be quite high. For example, Coinbase fees can be upwards of 10-13% on a transfer, but if you use their associated site, GDAX, there are no crypto-transfer or withdrawal fees (just a learning curve, which may make paying a fee on Coinbase worth the simplicity).

Payment Methods – What payment methods are available on the exchange? Credit & debit card? Wire transfer? PayPal? Bank Transfer? Bank transfers and Bank direct deposits can take a week to transfer. However, using Credit Cards can put you at a higher risk for fraud, so tread cautiously.

Verification Requirements – The vast majority of the Bitcoin trading platforms both in the US and the UK require some ID verification to make deposits & withdrawals. Some exchanges will allow you to remain anonymous. Although verification, which can take up to a few days, might be frustrating, it protects the exchange against all kinds of scams and money laundering.

Exchange Rate – Different exchanges have different rates. See figures below to see variable exchange prices.

Trading Pairs

LET'S RETURN TO THE SHOE-SHOPPING ANALOGY for the sake of understanding trading pairs. Essentially, if you wanted to buy a pair of shoes, which we will now call PAIR1, using US Dollars, the trading pair would be written as the following: PAIR1/USD. One could imagine if you went to another country, which used two different currencies like in Mexico for example, that there would be two trading pairs: PAIR1/USD and PAIR1/MXN (where MXN is Mexican Pesos). In crypto, the primary trading currency is Bitcoin (BTC). Therefore, if you wanted to buy Iota (MIOTA), the trading pair would be IOTA/BTC. See below for Iota's other trading pairs. These trading pairs can be found on CMC when you click on the coin of your choosing (open coin details and scroll down). See next figure.

IOTA Markets

#	Source	Pair	Volume (24h)	Price	Volume (%)	Updated
1	Bitfinex	MIOTA/USD	$39,548,600	$1.76	47.71%	Recently
2	Coinone	IOTA/KRW	$13,842,500	$1.78	16.70%	Recently
3	Bitfinex	MIOTA/BTC	$9,083,540	$1.78	10.96%	Recently
4	Binance	IOTA/BTC	$8,892,570	$1.79	10.73%	Recently
5	Binance	IOTA/ETH	$4,408,900	$1.79	5.32%	Recently
6	Bitfinex	MIOTA/ETH	$2,323,210	$1.77	2.80%	Recently
7	OKEx	IOTA/BTC	$1,760,820	$1.77	2.12%	Recently
8	Bitfinex	MIOTA/EUR	$1,582,050	$1.77	1.91%	Recently
9	OKEx	IOTA/USDT	$666,597	$1.76	0.80%	Recently
10	Binance	IOTA/BNB	$379,153	$1.77	0.46%	Recently
11	OKEx	IOTA/ETH	$136,536	$1.76	0.16%	Recently
12	Exrates	MIOTA/USD	$83,856	$1.79	0.10%	Recently
13	Exrates	MIOTA/BTC	$76,425	$1.76	0.09%	Recently
14	Gate.io	IOTA/USDT	$55,443	$1.84	0.07%	Recently
15	Gate.io	IOTA/BTC	$36,169	$1.81	0.04%	Recently
16	CoinFalcon	IOT/BTC	$9,434	$1.81	0.01%	Recently

One should note that the better exchanges tend to have more trading pairs listed, with exceptions, of course.

The chart on the following page shows the top 10 Exchanges/Markets based on 24h Volume on September 22, 2018. This is a snapshot to provide an example. These figures change daily.

WALLETS

WHERE DO I KEEP MY INTANGIBLE CURRENCY? This is a question that is on everyone's mind, especially the ones who are concerned about the safety of their currency on the blockchain. There are a few types of wallets used to store your coins. Each wallet, however, has their own security issues. Therefore, they are probably best chosen based on your personality and currency volume. Remember, currency security is all about the keys! Remember the homing pigeon?

Below are the six major types of wallets:

Online

Software

Mobile

Hardware

Paper

#	Name	Adj. Vol (24h)*	Volume (24h)	Volume (7d)	Volume (30d)	No. Markets	Change (24h)	Vol Graph (7d)	Launched
1	Binance	$2,326,592,121	$2,326,592,121	$8,074,911,616	$32,620,253,632	383	27.86%		Jul 2017
2	OKEx	$1,289,933,977	$1,289,933,977	$5,258,006,144	$24,382,675,264	509	20.54%		Jan 2014
3	Huobi	$1,092,982,524	$1,092,982,524	$4,538,143,808	$18,930,702,944	278	13.82%		Sep 2013
4	Bitfinex	$1,014,606,749	$1,014,606,749	$3,862,065,936	$14,437,397,088	84	-4.82%		Oct 2012
5	Upbit	$985,493,815	$986,084,785	$2,353,420,480	$5,802,590,144	269	49.94%		Oct 2017
6	Bithumb	$915,622,115	$915,622,115	$3,042,726,720	$11,378,986,832	46	24.99%		Jun 2016
7	ZB.COM	$450,225,859	$450,225,859	$2,487,269,504	$10,322,802,320	78	-3.39%		Nov 2017
8	HitBTC	$428,225,230	$428,227,232	$1,871,733,280	$8,218,622,720	786	24.87%		Feb 2014
9	DigiFinex	$421,049,444	$421,049,444	$1,194,577,784	$3,967,076,808	82	38.15%		Apr 2018
10	Bibox	$341,458,666	$341,458,666	$1,505,391,600	$6,009,789,536	202	5.69%		Nov 2017

Top 10 Exchanges/Markets based on 24h Volume on September 22, 2018

Online wallets: These wallets are hosted online in a cloud server, which are pretty user-friendly. One downside of this is having to trust a third party with your private keys. Something else to consider is that not all online wallets can hold all the different alt-coins/tokens, therefore you will need multiple wallets to manage all of your currencies. Coinbase, for example only holds, Bitcoin (BTC), Bitcoin Cash (BCH), Etherium (ETH), Litecoin (LTC) and your home currency, in my case, US Dollars. You will have to find a wallet that is compatible with the coins you want to store, or you may just have to keep them on the exchange.

Some examples of online wallets are Coinbase, Exodus, Coinpayments, & Bitstamp.

Software wallet: Software wallets are more secure than online wallets, however, they still require some frequent updating depending on who makes the wallet. Even though you have better care and security for your keys on these wallets, if you aren't very tech-savvy, then you should probably opt-out of the desktop wallets all together. Let me give you an example. Some coins allow you to stake their coins. Which means, if you get in early enough, usually pre-ICO, you can earn coins by holding them in their proprietary wallet, which needs to stay open 24/7 on a running computer and requires manual, mandatory updates to prevent losing your coins. The issues that I faced with one particular coin went like this:

This specific coin's wallet was calling for upgrades every 7-10 days, which meant, I had to back up my wallet carefully or risk losing my coins. Sounds easy enough, until I realized the steps required for this to take place (with this specific wallet): First, I needed to find the program folder on my computer for the appropriate wallet and locate the *wallet.dat* file. This needed to be held in a safe place, such as a folder elsewhere on your system because if this gets lost, I would've lost all of my coins! Next, I needed to download 2-3 other *.config* files from specific sites that were given to me and other stake holders in private discussion groups, of which I had to find and join. Once I downloaded all of the appropriate files and saved my *wallet.dat* file, I had to place the files back in the folder and exchange the newly downloaded *wallet.dat* for the saved one, restart the program and hope that my currency showed up.

If you keep your public and private keys on your computer system and fail to copy them elsewhere, and your computer gets stolen, your coins will be lost forever. Unfortunately, there isn't a tech support that can help you with this. Don't lose your keys!

Another (stress-related) issue is the fact that once you download the wallet; it has to download EACH and EVERY transaction that *has ever been recorded* in the entire ledger (blockchain). The last wallet I downloaded took almost two weeks to download every transaction until I could verify that the currency that I recently sent was in my wallet! As you could imagine, this can cause a lot of anxiety – especially if you made a large deposit/purchase.

Mobile wallets: Mobile wallets are available as apps for your smartphone, especially useful if you want to pay for something using bitcoin in a store or online shop. All of the online wallets and most of the desktop ones mentioned above have mobile versions. Mobile wallets are becoming a growing genre for crypto-developers at the moment.

Some examples include Electrum (Android), Mycelium (Android, iOS), Coinobi (Android, iOS), Mobi (Android, iOS), Coinbase (Android, iOS). Ethos.

Hardware wallets: Hardware wallets are extremely secure, as they are offline (cold wallets) and therefore not hackable. Essentially they are fancy, secure thumb drives. One downfall is they can be stolen or lost along with the Bitcoin and other currencies stored on them. Some large investors keep their hardware wallets (and paper wallets – see below) in secure locations such as bank vaults. *Some examples include: Trezor, Keepkey and Ledger, and Case*

Paper wallets: Perhaps the simplest of all the wallets. These are pieces of paper on which the private and public keys of a bitcoin address are printed. They contain all information about your currency so if it gets lost, so does your currency. This type of wallet is ideal for long-term storage in a bank vault or safe deposit box (away from fire or water damage), as well as, giving this currency as a gift. These are most secure because they are cold (not on the internet).

You can easily create a paper wallet from home where you can print it, fold it, seal it and store it away safely. *Some examples of services include: WalletGenerator and BitcoinPaperWallet*

Exchange Wallets? Sometimes wallets are not compatible with all of the coins that you have, requiring you to keep the imcompatible coins on the exchange and pray that it doesn't get hacked. That's just the way it is.

Portfolio Managers:

ONCE YOU HAVE PURCHASED YOUR LOAD OF COINS, you will want a central location where you can visualize current, up-to-date information about each of your coins. Therefore, you will want to use a portfolio manager. There are plenty of options, and since most people own a smartphone with the ability to install apps, having a portfolio manager on your phone is likely the most common and efficient option. There are a few portfolio managers that obtain the information directly from individual exchanges (saving the manual input process), but once again, this is for the tech-savvy ones, and still may not work with all of your exchanges, therefore, I will skip this topic.

Portfolio manager apps and programs work by manual entry of your coins and the cost of BTC (or ETH) that you spent to purchase the coin. The purchase price is compared against the current price of the coin and will show you gains or losses.

There are plenty of online and mobile portfolio managers, yet there are only a select few which most cryptophiles use - one, in particular, is Blockfolio:

Blockfolio is undoubtedly the most popular mobile portfolio (I am not shilling this software). Its design is simple. It has integrated news from your chosen sources, the ability to watch a coin (put on your portfolio without having to have purchased it), and add alerts for when a coin hits a limit for which you want to sell or buy. It's clean, easy and gives lots of information.

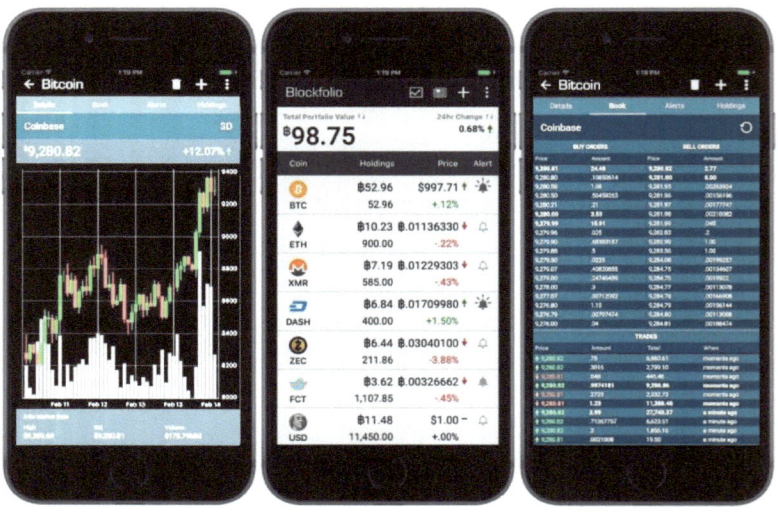

There are plenty of other portfolios, so just search your app store for crypto portfolio and see what works for you.

STRATEGIES:

SO, YOU'VE MANAGED TO GET TO THIS POINT, and I'm sure you are starting to have questions, theories or predictions about a coin's potential value. When I started, I bought a coin (we will call Coin-X) whose value was $.0000254 per coin. The circulating supply was around 600 million, which is high (not much room to grow). I thought to myself, "Wow, if this coin goes to 10 cents, based on my $300 investment, I will make $1.18 Million!" I was stoked. Then, I started understanding market capitalization based on comparable coins, or at least Bitcoin, and was rudely awakened. The *market cap* is the mathematical product of the Circulating supply and the Current Price per coin/token:

$$MC = total\ circulating\ supply\ x\ current\ coin\ price$$

Once I understood this, I knew that price prediction had to be based on realistic projections, not just wishful thinking. For example, Bitcoin's current Market Cap (MC) is $153 Billion. So for Coin-X to reach my wishful, yet unrealistic $1.18 million return, it would have to grow 3937 times, which we would yield a market cap of $2.4 Trillion, which is 15x greater than Bitcoin. It's just not reasonable. Ideally, when we are trying to forecast a coin's predictive value we should compare market caps with a coin that is similar. In this case, I used Bitcoin to prove a point because it is the highest market cap of all cryptocurrency. So, to be 15 times higher than Bitcoin in its market capitalization would make this growth virtually impossible. Let's do that math to see how I came up with these numbers.

Refer to the above paragraphs – I will start at the top:

Wishful price ($0.10) divided by current coin price:

($0.10 / .0000254) = 3937

This 3937 is the Multiplier (Mp), therefore,

Investment x Mp = Worth (based on investment), or

$300 x 3937 = $1.18 Million (and some change).

MC of Bitcoin = $153 Billion – found on coinmarketcap or equivalent site which is calculated by:

MC = 16,917,112 Coins in circulation X $9075 current BTC price

So, Taking the Mp (3937) X Market Cap of Coin-X,

you get $2.4 Trillion.

Thus, $2.4 Trillion / $153 Billion = 15, which represents Coin-X's 15X increase in market cap compared to Bitcoin.

This type of hyped, deluded, and over-estimated speculation happens all the time. Take Ripple (XRP) for example – Its current market cap is $30.5 Billion. Many people speculate (or simply hope) that Ripple will go to $50 per coin. One can easily see how far-fetched this hopeful projection is when we do the math:

MC of XRP = $30.5 Billion

To go to $50 per coin, we need to figure out the Multiplier (Mp) which is Wishful price divided by the current price:

$50 / $0.78 = 64 Mp.

Now, take this Multiplier and multiply it times the current MC (market cap) of XRP (64 x $30.5B = 1.92 Trillion.)

This is 12.5 x more than Bitcoin, calculated by dividing $192 Trillion / $153 Billion

So, when asked if Ripple will hit $50, you can confidently exclaim, in your best British accent, "Rubbish!" with a clear explanation.

If you didn't get quite understand the math, review it again from the beginning until it all makes clear sense. It's much simpler once you know the basics.

part 2
let's buy some coins

Make sure to refer to earlier sections in the book to understand what task you are doing and why it's essential. In this section, I figured the best way to guide you through the steps would be via a checklist. The checklist will be broken down into sections to make it easier to find topics later. Good luck.

BUYING YOUR FIRST BITCOIN USING YOUR HOME CURRENCY

1. Have a smart-phone available as you may need to verify via SMS. Also, you may be required to take a picture of yourself holding your driver's license or other written information on paper for other accounts.

2. Establish an account with a site that can exchange your currency for Bitcoin (BTC)

3. For this example, let's use Coinbase: www.Coinbase.com

    4. Once you've established your account, If asked, make sure to check your email to validate/activate it. Be sure to CHECK YOUR SPAM folder if you don't see it.

5. Have your credit card, debit card or bank account routing and account numbers available. Remember, using a bank account will take up to 9 days for the money to arrive in your wallet after the purchase, whereas using a Credit Card (CC) or debit card will be immediate, and you can make a purchase within minutes.

    a. Don't buy more than you are willing to lose!

6. Remember, you can buy in fractions of BTC, or just enter your country's currency amount, and it will be calculated into the BTC fraction.

    a. For example - $100 at current BTC value is worth 0.01238 BTC

7. Now that the money is in your BTC wallet, leave it if you want to hold BTC or send it to another exchange to buy ALT-coins.

8. Next time you log in (or the first time), Coinbase will send you a 2-factor authentication code to your mobile phone via test message. Enter this number on the Coinbase website (if prompted).

9. If you want to use Coinbase to send coins to an exchange to purchase alt-coins, follow the next set of steps. Of note, there will be higher fees using Coinbase (as opposed to GDAX – its big brother affiliate), but the steps are easier. If you don't want to

spend more on fees and are okay adding a few extra steps which require more tech-savviness, then proceed to step 17

SENDING CURRENCY TO EXCHANGE – NOT GDAX (If using Coinbase).

10. After your coins are purchased, click on ACCOUNTS at the top of the screen. You will see the list of all accounts on Coinbase. The first one is usually BTC account. For this instruction, we will use BTC, but this is essentially the same information for any coin on Coinbase.

11. You should see your BTC Wallet with its amount, home currency equivalent and 3 buttons: SEND, RECEIVE and Ellipsis (3-DOTS). If you click on the ellipsis, you can rename this account.

12. **STOP HERE**. Skip to step 25 to obtain deposit address - this occurs specifically around step 35

13. At this point you want to SEND your coins to an exchange where you can purchase your alt-coins. Click SEND

    14. A new window will pop up with a few boxes to fill in:

        a. Recipient: Enter the email address of the receiver or the BITCOIN address of where you will be sending your coins. If you are sending to an exchange to buy alt-coins, you will need the BTC DEPOSIT ADDRESS on the exchange where you will be purchasing.

b. Amount of Bitcoin to send

c. Optional message – some exchanges will require this, although it's rare.

15. CLICK SEND FUNDS once you have entered all the appropriate and correct information – triple check this!

16. Now, just be patient and check your account on the exchange where you sent the coins for your deposit. This may take 15-60 minutes depending on Blockchain traffic.

SENDING CURRENCY TO GDAX
(If using Coinbase)

This requires intermediate to advanced tech skills

17. Why use GDAX? GDAX has no transfer fees! Coinbase has high transfer fees (not when sending to GDAX)! Remember GDAX is the big-brother affiliate to Coinbase.

18. Go to www.GDAX.com. If you are logged into Coinbase already, you will automatically be logged in when you click "login." If not, it will prompt you for your Coinbase password.

19. Once logged in, for now, ignore all the details in the middle and right of the screen and focus on the left 2 inches – top to bottom.

20. On the upper left, next to the GDAX logo, make sure "select product" is set to BTC/USD (it's a pull-down menu) – or ETH/USD if you are sending Etherium from Coinbase. Recall trading pairs.

21. Now click DEPOSIT on the left, and then click COINBASE ACCOUNT on the new popup window.

22. If it's not populated already, enter the BTC amount that you want to transfer in the AMOUNT box (this can be found on the left side of the screen, BALANCE.)

23. Click DEPOSIT FUNDS. (This puts Coinbase BTC into the GDAX Wallet).

-STOP-

24. At this point, you need to establish an account with an exchange to buy alt-coins before we can send currency from GDAX)

ESTABLISH AN ACCOUNT WITH AN ALT-COIN EXCHANGE

Even though many exchanges appear different and may appear confusing at first glance, once you figure one out, you should be able to figure out the others. Let's begin.

25. Head over to the ALT-COIN exchange of your desire. Let's say the coin you want is on Kucoin, (www.kucoin.com). Let's take you through the process.

26. Before you start, you will need to download the *Google Authenticator* from your mobile app store (available for both android and iOS).

27. SIGN UP (upper right-hand corner of website).

28. Enter the appropriate information – EMAIL and PASSWORD with Confirmation.

29. A confirmation email will be sent to the email address you used at signup. Click it.

30. You should then be directed back to KuCoin to validate your account. You are done. Congratulations.

31. At this point, you are ready to go, but for increased security, I would add an extra layer of protection to your account to prevent fraud and theft.

32. On the left, click the link for *Google 2-step* (Google Authentication). Follow the directions from there.

33. So, let's get some currency to this account so you can buy your ALT-COINs

34. Every exchange is different, but the following deposit process is quite similar to most exchanges. Some are more difficult to negotiate, while others are quite simple.

35. When you log in, you will be taken to the OVERVIEW section (you can also click on the "$" sign on the upper right corner of the screen). A considerable list will be present with all the coins that THIS exchange offers. Notice on the right that there are two links, DEPOSIT & WITHDRAWAL, look above that column, and you will also see a SEARCH COIN area.

36. Click SEARCH COIN and Type BTC. Hit enter.

37. You will see multiple coins pop up with BTC or variations of BTC. Find BTC and follow that row to the right and click the associated DEPOSIT link.

38. Click CONFIRM that you want to deposit into BTC. This is important!

39. Now, you will see a bunch of numbers and letters looking a lot like this (this is the BTC deposit address):

    1MZzvhaaPWrsw267dsgzXpHud13JKtedzDGec

40. EACH COIN has its unique address. But you will mostly only deposit BTC or ETH unless you are transferring an ALT-Coin from one exchange to another. If this is the case, repeat the search coin feature for the alt-coin you want and get THAT deposit address.

41. COPY THIS EXACTLY by selecting the first to last digit. *IMPORTANT! Make sure you are NOT selecting a blank space before or after the address.*

93jd93jdoslsjeje9ossksjdkv

Wrong. Notice the empty spaces after the last letters?

Correct. Notice there are no empty spaces after the last letters.

This has to be EXACT, so when you send currency, it gets to the appropriate address. Once sent, you cannot correct it, and you will lose your money it if the address is wrong.

-STOP –
Return to GDAX

42. On GDAX, on the left side of the screen, click WITHDRAWAL.

43. A new window will open. Click BTC ADDRESS.

44. Now, enter an amount to send from your earlier deposit and PASTE your BTC deposit address from Kucoin or your other exchange.

45. Under this, there is a "Two- Factor Code" to complete the deposit.

46. Click GET CODE. It will come to your phone via text message. Typically, it is seven numbers. Enter that in the window.

47. DOUBLE CHECK your address and amount.

48. Click, WITHDRAW FUNDS.

49. Within 15 minutes to 1 hour, your funds will arrive in your exchange.

50. Be patient. They will arrive if you have followed all the steps correctly!

LET'S BUY SOME ALT-COINS!

51. After the coins have arrived, they can be stored on the exchange or used to purchase coins or tokens. Click on MARKETS at the top of the screen

52. Go to the SEARCH box and type the name of the coin you want to buy. Let's Choose NEO (basically this is the Chinese equivalent Etherium). Search NEO and make sure you choose NEO/BTC (see "trading pairs" earlier). This means you will be trading NEO for BTC. Clicking this will open the trading window.

53. THIS PART CAN BE OVERWHELMING! DO NOT BE INTIMIDATED BY THIS. Notice when this loads, you will see the chart on the left, the buy and sell order books on the right and the ordering window is below that.

54. To access the trading, enter your 2-factor Authentication from your new Google Authenticator application from your smartphone if asked

55. In most trading windows there are two sides, a BUYING SIDE, and a SELLING SIDE. The BUYING side is usually set up as best price on the top to low price on the bottom. Some sites, like Kucoin, have a BEST PRICE button in the

ordering area - this *best price* is essentially a MARKET ORDER (see below).

56. Above where you type the order, there is hyperlink text that reads AVAILABLE BTC, which shows how much available BTC you have to use. TO USE IT ALL, CLICK THE AMOUNT and it will be placed in the BUY area.

a. If you don't want to use it all, use the RATIO slider to choose the fraction that you want to use..

57. You can now purchase the coin by clicking BUY, and it will show up in the OVERVIEW section, which is seen at login or by clicking the Dollar sign in the upper right-hand corner.

58. There are two ways to purchase your coins:

>b. **MARKET ORDER** - Simplest and Quickest. This is the best price on the market. You will buy whatever the next available best-price is. For example, if someone is selling 100 coins and you buy 145 coins, you will buy the best price from the first person selling 100 coins and the remaining 45 will be purchased at the next best price available. These two prices could be different depending on the market values.

c. **LIMIT ORDER** - More difficult and requires patience. This is where you set a limit to either buy or sell your coins at a specified price. For example, if 100 people are selling their coins at $60 and you decide that you won't sell until it's $75 then you can make that happen. All that's needed is a price surge, excitement, and patience. You can also choose to set a limit to buy or sell a coin at a lower price point, but you may wait as well!

59. Oh yeah…HODL!

GLOSSARY OF TERMS

2-factor authentication (2-FA) – A method used to increase security for logging into websites, usually by entering specific data either generated by an application on smartphone or another bit of information

A Satoshi - Currently the smallest unit of the bitcoin currency recorded on the block chain. It is a one hundred millionth of a single bitcoin (0.00000001 BTC). It is named after the original founder of Bitcoin, Satoshi Nakamoto.

Airdrop - A procedure of distributing tokens by awarding them to existing holders of a particular blockchain currency.

Alt-coins – any coin that isn't Bitcoin or Etherium

ATH - All Time High

Bear (-ish) Market - a market in which prices are falling, encouraging selling.

Blockchain – A continuously growing list of records, called blocks, which are linked and secured using cryptography

BTC –Call letters for Bitcoin on exchanges

BTC Dominance – The Market share of Bitcoin against all coins measured as a percentage using Market cap

BTFD – "Buy The Fucking Dip" – Encouraging to buy when people are selling off their coins

Bull (-ish) Market - A market in which share prices are rising, encouraging buying.

Circulating supply – The estimated amount of coins or tokens in circulation at the given moment

Coins – Unlike Tokens, Coins are used as a currency, solely

Cryptocurrency – A valued asset that is used for trade and safe-guarded by encryption techniques

DDoS – Abbreviation for Distributed Denial of Service. A DDoS is a cyber attack utilizing many different computers to tie up the resources of a website or web service.

Deposit Address – The address where you will send or receive coins from one exchange or wallet to another.

DYOR – Do Your Own Research

FIAT currency – Paper Money

FOMO – Fear Of Missing Out

FUD – Fear, Uncertainty and Doubt

Google Authenticator App – A Smartphone app, which generates a random 6 digit code proprietary to the specific exchange you need to log in to. Used for 2-factor Authentication (2-FA).

Hash functions – Mathematical equations solved by node computers to validate ledger transactions before they can be placed into the blockchain

HODL – Hold On For Dear Life

ICO – Initial Coin Offering (Like IPO in stocks)

Limit Order – An order to purchase or sell where you set the selling price

Long – To take a *long-position* on a coin is to believe the price will rise in the future.

Market Capitalization (Market Cap) – The total Value of a coin based on the product of the Circulating Supply and the current crypto price. MC = CS x Current Crypto Price

Market Order – An order to purchase crypto at the current best price on the exchange

Miner(s) – A person who owns or rents a computer (node) that is used to solve HASH functions to earn cryptocurrency (and help support the bitcoin), usually Bitcoin.

MtGOX – A large coin exchange which was hacked in 201 for 815,000 Bitcoin!

Multiplier – In crypto, the higher the better. It represents how many times a coin has multiplied from a certain point in time. For example: CoinX=$1 per coin. 3 months ago it was $.005 per coin. Therefore, the multiplier is 200 or 200x

Portfolio Manager – An app or program tracks cryptocurrency's progress

Private key – An individual key that can encrypt or decrypt information. This must be kept safe.

Public key – Just like the private key, but the public key can be made public to allow others to validate you and your transaction.

Pump and Dump – A form of securities fraud that involves artificially inflating the price of an owned stock through false and misleading positive statements, in order to sell the cheaply purchased stock at a higher price.

Satoshi Nakamoto – The enigmatic and assumed founder of Bitcoin

Shilling – The act of Influential traders publicly rooting for a rise in the coin in hopes of igniting the public's interest in that particular coin without divulging their personal interest.

Shit-coin – An alt-coin that becomes worthless over time

Short – To take a *short-position* on a coin is to anticipate a drop in a coin's value

Technical Analysis (TA) – Using graphical objective data and tools to predict a coins movement, pattern and future shifts. Mostly used in Stocks.

To moon or mooning – An extreme Bull market or a huge multiplier over s short period of time.

Token – Unlike a Coin, Tokens have a utility function more than just digital currency

Total supply – The maximum supply that a coin will ever have, which is different than circulating supply.

Wallets – A digital, paper or hardware location where information about your coins are kept

Yarl – A 1990's term, which illustrates the vocal styles of alternative rock.

List of top 200 Coins Ranked by Total Market Capitalization As of March 2018

1. Bitcoin (BTC)
2. Ethereum (ETH)
3. Ripple (XRP)
4. Bitcoin Cash (BCH)
5. Litecoin (LTC)
6. Cardano (ADA)
7. NEO (NEO)
8. Stellar (XLM)
9. EOS (EOS)
10. Monero (XMR)
11. IOTA (MIOTA)
12. Dash (DASH)
13. NEM (XEM)
14. Tether (USDT)
15. TRON (TRX)
16. VeChain (VEN)
17. Ethereum Classic (ETC)
18. Lisk (LSK)
19. Nano (NANO)
20. Bitcoin Gold (BTG)
21. OmiseGo (OMG)
22. Qtum (QTUM)
23. Binance Coin (BNB)
24. Zcash (ZEC)
25. ICON (ICX)
26. DigixDAO (DGD)
27. Populous (PPT)
28. Waves (WAVES)
29. Steem (STEEM)
30. Bytecoin (BCN)
31. Verge (XVG)
32. Maker (MKR)

33. Stratis (STRAT)
34. RChain (RHOC)
35. Dogecoin (DOGE)
36. BitShares (BTS)
37. Aeternity (AE)
38. Decred (DCR)
39. Augur (REP)
40. Siacoin (SC)
41. Bytom (BTM)
42. Status (SNT)
43. Ontology (ONT)
44. Waltonchain (WTC)
45. Zilliqa (ZIL)
46. Komodo (KMD)
47. Ardor (ARDR)
48. Ark (ARK)
49. Cryptonex (CNX)
50. Aion (AION)
51. 0x (ZRX)
52. Veritaseum (VERI)
53. Hshare (HSR)
54. Electroneum (ETN)
55. MonaCoin (MONA)
56. PIVX (PIVX)
57. DigiByte (DGB)
58. KuCoin Shares (KCS)
59. Factom (FCT)
60. SysCoin (SYS)
61. Basic Attention Token (BAT)
62. Golem (GNT)
63. Gas (GAS)
64. Revain (R)
65. Ethos (ETHOS)
66. QASH (QASH)
67. Nebulas (NAS)
68. Loopring (LRC)
69. FunFair (FUN)

70. Dragonchain (DRGN)
71. Emercoin (EMC)
72. GXChain (GXS)
73. ZCoin (XZC)
74. aelf (ELF)
75. IOStoken (IOST)
76. ReddCoin (RDD)
77. Kyber Network (KNC)
78. Kin (KIN)
79. Dentacoin (DCN)
80. SALT (SALT)
81. ChainLink (LINK)
82. SmartCash (SMART)
83. Nxt (NXT)
84. MaidSafeCoin (MAID)
85. Cindicator (CND)
86. Byteball Bytes (GBYTE)
87. Power Ledger (POWR)
88. Polymath Network (POLY)
89. Bancor (BNT)
90. Particl (PART)
91. TenX (PAY)
92. Neblio (NEBL)
93. Request Network (REQ)
94. Nucleus Vision (NCASH)
95. Iconomi (ICN)
96. SIRIN LABS Token (SRN)
97. Dent (DENT)
98. Nexus (NXS)
99. MinexCoin (MNX)
100. Bitcore (BTX)
101. Pillar (PLR)
102. Storj (STORJ)
103. BitcoinDark (BTCD)
104. SingularityNET (AGI)

105. Genesis Vision (GVT)
106. Decentraland (MANA)
107. Gnosis (GNO)
108. Vertcoin (VTC)
109. Substratum (SUB)
110. Blocknet (BLOCK)
111. Achain (ACT)
112. Theta Token (THETA)
113. Civic (CVC)
114. Dynamic Trading Rights (DTR)
115. Raiden Network Token (RDN)
116. Storm (STORM)
117. Quantstamp (QSP)
118. GameCredits (GAME)
119. Enjin Coin (ENJ)
120. Monaco (MCO)
121. iExec RLC (RLC)
122. Santiment Network Token (SAN)
123. Metal (MTL)
124. Ignis (IGNIS)
125. Aragon (ANT)
126. SaluS (SLS)
127. Genaro Network (GNX)
128. Ubiq (UBQ)
129. Experience Points (XP)
130. Po.et (POE)
131. ZenCash (ZEN)
132. Skycoin (SKY)
133. WAX (WAX)
134. NAV Coin (NAV)
135. Asch (XAS)
136. Envion (EVN)
137. PayPie (PPP)
138. XPA (XPA)
139. Arcblock (ABT)

140. POA Network (POA)
141. BridgeCoin (BCO)
142. Time New Bank (TNB)
143. Bibox Token (BIX)
144. Pura (PURA)
145. Oyster (PRL)
146. High Performance Blockchain (HPB)
147. SophiaTX (SPHTX)
148. DigitalNote (XDN)
149. DEW (DEW)
150. Nuls (NULS)
151. Credits (CS)
152. Cube (AUTO)
153. Edgeless (EDG)
154. AdEx (ADX)
155. Bluzelle (BLZ)
156. BLOCKv (VEE)
157. Einsteinium (EMC2)
158. ION (ION)
159. Fusion (FSN)
160. EthLend (LEND)
161. Feathercoin (FTC)
162. MediShares (MDS)
163. Medibloc (MED)
164. CRYPTO20 (C20)
165. Streamr DATAcoin (DATA)
166. SpankChain (SPANK)
167. Quantum Resistant Ledger (QRL)
168. Telcoin (TEL)
169. Jibrel Network (JNT)
170. CyberMiles (CMT)
171. BitBay (BAY)
172. Simple Token (OST)
173. Ripio Credit Network (RCN)

174. Universa (UTNP)
175. Pundi X (PSX)
176. Wagerr (WGR)
177. Peercoin (PPC)
178. SONM (SNM)
179. XtraBYtes (XBY)
180. SmartMesh (SMT)
181. Ambrosus (AMB)
182. Red Pulse (RPX)
183. Eidoo (EDO)
184. TaaS (TAAS)
185. Wings (WINGS)
186. OriginTrail (TRAC)
187. SpaceChain (SPC)
188. Gifto (GTO)
189. VIBE (VIBE)
190. Ink (INK)
191. AppCoins (APPC)
192. LBRY Credits (LBC)
193. IoT Chain (ITC)
194. HTMLCOIN (HTML)
195. KickCoin (KICK)
196. NAGA (NGC)
197. SingularDTV (SNGLS)
198. DeepBrain Chain (DBC)
199. Melon (MLN)
200. Gulden (NL

I am not a financial planner and this is not financial advice.
DO YOUR OWN RESEARCH
GOOD LUCK & HODL

www.ingramcontent.com/pod-product-compliance
Lightning Source LLC
Chambersburg PA
CBHW041524090426
42737CB00038B/109